3 wk

KT-583-357

Biography.

Ellen R. Butts and Joyce R. Schwartz

Lerner Publications Company
Minneapolis

This book is available in two editions:
Library binding by Lerner Publications Company,
a division of Lerner Publishing Group
Soft cover by First Avenue Editions,
an imprint of Lerner Publishing Group
241 First Avenue North
Minneapolis, MN 55401 U.S.A.

Website address: www.lernerbooks.com

Library of Congress Cataloging-in-Publication Data

Butts, Ellen.
    Fidel Castro / by Ellen R. Butts and Joyce R. Schwartz.
       p.   cm. — (A&E biography)
    Includes bibliographical references and index.
    ISBN: 0–8225–2371–X (lib. bdg. : alk. paper)
    ISBN: 0–8225–9524–9 (pbk. : alk. paper)
    1. Castro, Fidel, 1926—Juvenile literature. 2. Heads of state—Cuba—
Biography—Juvenile literature. 3. Revolutionaries—Cuba—Biography—
Juvenile literature. 4. Cuba—History—1933–1959—Juvenile literature.
5. Cuba—History—1959—Juvenile literature. I. Schwartz, Joyce R.
II. Title. III. Series: Biography (Lerner Publications Company)
F1788.22.C3B87 2005
972.9106'4'092—dc22   2004017908

Manufactured in the United States of America
1 2 3 4 5 6 – JR – 10 09 08 07 06 05

CONTENTS

The first page of the letter young Fidel Castro wrote to President Franklin D. Roosevelt in 1940. In the letter, Fidel says he is twelve, though he actually wrote the letter when he was fourteen.

INTRODUCTION: A LETTER

On November 6, 1940, Fidel Castro wrote a letter to Franklin Delano Roosevelt. Fidel was a fourteen-year-old student at a boarding school in Santiago de Cuba, Cuba. Franklin Roosevelt had just been reelected to a third term as president of the United States. In shaky English, Fidel wrote, "My good friend Roosevelt I don't know very English, but I know as much as write to you." He congratulated Roosevelt on his reelection and asked him to "give me a ten dollars bill green American . . . because never, I have not seen a ten dollars bill green American and I would like to have one of them. . . . Thank you very much. Good by. Your friend. Fidel Castro." In a postscript, he offered, "If you want iron to make your ships, I will show to you the biggest (minos) of iron of the land."

In 1940 President Roosevelt was faced with many world-shaking crises. The United States was still reeling from the Great Depression, a severe economic downturn that began in 1929 and lasted until the early 1940s and caused widespread unemployment and hardship. World War II (1939–1945) had begun the previous year when Germany invaded Poland, and the growing conflict already involved many nations. Roosevelt didn't have time to pay attention to the personal request of an unknown boy from a small island in the Caribbean Sea.

Jobless men wait in a breadline for free coffee and doughnuts during the Great Depression. Such lines were common in the United States during this era.

A dollar was a lot of money in 1940. In the United States, it could buy ten cups of coffee or twenty large candy bars. In Cuba everything cost even less. Fidel's allowance was eighty cents a month. But he didn't ask the president for just one dollar—he wanted ten. From the time he was a young child, Fidel demanded more, reached further, and thought bigger than anyone else.

Twenty years after writing that letter, the ambitious schoolboy became leader and then dictator of Cuba. Ten U.S. presidents have held office since Castro took power in 1959. Each of them has had to contend with Castro and his tiny island nation. Cuba has been a source of frustration, tension, and even danger to its much larger neighbor to the north. In Cuba and abroad, Fidel is loved and hated, revered and despised. But he remains endlessly fascinating.

Castro excelled in basketball during his school years and was named best athlete of Belén College in 1945.

Chapter **ONE**

A HEADSTRONG BOY

THE LARGE, HEALTHY BOY WAS BORN ON AUGUST 13, 1926, in Birán, a small farm community in southeastern Cuba. His parents named him Fidel, after a wealthy local politician. Fidel Alejandro Castro Ruz was the third of seven children born to Ángel Castro y Argiz and his second wife, Lina Ruz González. Ángel also had two older children from his first marriage.

FIDEL'S PARENTS

Ángel Castro came from Galicia, a poor region in northwestern Spain. His family couldn't afford to own any land. They lived in a one-room stone house above their cows and pigs. Realizing he had no future in Galicia, Ángel made his way to Oriente Province in southeastern

Cuba in the early 1900s. He arrived just as Cuba was becoming an independent nation after four hundred years as a Spanish colony. Colonial rule had ended with Spain's defeat in the Spanish-American War in 1898. In that conflict, the United States fought Spain to free Cuba from Spanish control. Before becoming an independent republic, Cuba was under U.S. military control from 1898 to 1902.

Ángel Castro was tall, strong, hardworking, and determined to be successful. At first, he cut sugarcane and laid railroad tracks for the United Fruit Company, a huge U.S. firm that controlled Cuba's most important business, sugar production and export (sale to foreign countries). Castro worked alongside the descendants of African slaves, as well as more recent immigrants from Haiti, Jamaica, and China. Later, he peddled lemonade to field-workers and cheap supplies to local farm families. Eventually, he saved enough money to buy land and hire his own workers. They planted and harvested sugarcane, which Castro sold to United Fruit, his former employer. He also taught himself to read and write.

Ángel became one of the wealthiest and most respected men in Oriente. He was known to his neighbors as Don Ángel Castro. He married a local schoolteacher, and they had two children, Pedro Emilio and Lidia. Then Ángel left his wife for their fifteen-year-old maid, Lina. Ángel and Lina had two children before Fidel: Ángela and Ramón. After Fidel came his younger brother Raúl and sisters Juana (called Juanita), Emma, and Agustina. When Ángel and Lina first started their family, they weren't married. They married several years after Fidel's birth.

By the time Fidel was born, Ángel owned or rented more than twenty-five thousand acres of land and supported three hundred families on his property in Birán. The Castros lived in a large, two-story wooden house propped up on stilts to make room underneath for the family's cows, pigs, and chickens. As his estate grew larger, Ángel built a repair shop, a general store, and a bakery. The only buildings in the area that he didn't own were the post office and the school.

Although Ángel had become a rich man, he worked hard and lived simply. He wore rough peasant clothes, shaved his head, and carried a silver-handled whip. He brought breakfast to his workers every day and was generous to them on holidays, but he had a fierce temper and was a demanding boss.

Like Ángel, Lina came from a very poor Spanish family and didn't learn to read or write until she was an adult. She was tall, wore traditional black clothing, and had an outgoing personality. She was also a deeply religious Roman Catholic. Even after she became a rich man's wife, Lina never thought of herself as a grand lady. She was happiest in the kitchen helping her Afro-Cuban maids cook the large meal of the day. When the food was ready, she summoned everyone to dinner with a blast from a shotgun.

CAREFREE CHILDHOOD

Ángel and Lina were loving parents, and Fidel had a happy childhood. He played with his brothers and sisters and the farmworkers' children. He later explained, "Where I was born and raised, we lived among poor people; all of the children went barefoot. . . . They were my friends and comrades in everything. . . . I did not belong to another social class." This was unusual in Cuba at the time. Normally, the children of wealthy landowners and poor peasants did not have much to do with each other. They came from two separate social groups and led very different lives.

Fidel was strong and athletic and loved being outdoors. He and his brothers, sisters, and friends climbed hills, swam in the river, and rode horses on the family estate. As Fidel grew older, he learned to use a shotgun, sometimes practicing his aim on his mother's hens.

Like his father, Fidel had a quick temper. If someone opposed him, he lashed out in violent tantrums. He couldn't bear to lose and always insisted on having his own way. After organizing a softball team and convincing his father to buy the bats, balls, and gloves, Fidel demanded to be the pitcher. But when his side began to lose, he would stop the game and go home.

At the age of four, Fidel entered the local public school with Ángela and Ramón, his older sister and brother. He learned to read and write by the time he was five, but his hot temper got him in trouble. In an interview many years later, he admitted, "I remember that whenever I disagreed with something the teacher said to me, or whenever I got mad, I would swear at her and immediately leave school, running as fast as I could."

SCHOOL IN SANTIAGO

When Fidel turned five, his parents decided to send him to Santiago de Cuba, the capital of Oriente Province, so that he could attend a better school. They arranged for him and Ángela to live with the Hibbert family, relatives of one of Fidel's teachers in Birán. Instead of sending Fidel to school, Mrs. Hibbert taught him arithmetic, spelling, and handwriting at home. The work was too easy for him, and he had no playmates. There wasn't enough food, even though Don Ángel paid the Hibberts to care for his children. Fidel was bored and hungry, and he let his parents know it.

The following year, Fidel returned to the Hibberts, but he attended first grade at La Salle, a Catholic boys' school. There was enough food, and classes and friends kept him busy, but he had begun to resent the Hibberts' strict rules. When Mr. Hibbert spanked him for misbehaving, Fidel threw a tantrum and demanded to live at La Salle School as a boarder. He got his way.

During Fidel's fourth year at La Salle, his brothers Ramón and Raúl joined him. But having his brothers there didn't improve Fidel's behavior. He fought with his classmates and hit back at one of the priests. Ángel received a report saying that his sons didn't study and were the worst bullies who had ever attended La Salle. That summer Ángel announced that the boys wouldn't be returning to school the next year.

When Fidel threatened to burn down the house if he couldn't go to school in Santiago, his father relented. Fidel entered fifth grade at Dolores College, a much better and more exclusive school that was run by the Jesuits, an order of Catholic priests known for their excellence as teachers. Many of the students came from wealthy, distinguished families and considered themselves superior to people who grew up on farms in the country. At Dolores the classes were harder and Fidel had trouble keeping up.

To make things worse, he hated his new home with a businessman who was his father's friend. Ángel sent money for a twenty-cent weekly allowance, but the man withheld it if Fidel didn't earn the highest grades. Fidel tricked him by showing him a fake report card with excellent grades, then forging the man's signature on the real one and returning it to the school.

When Fidel was ten, he had to have his appendix removed. The incision became infected, so Fidel was forced to stay in the hospital for three months. After being released, he returned to school and to the businessman's house. Fidel was constantly ordered to his room to study but wanted only "to do nothing, listen to the radio or go out." Finally, he told the man's family "all to go to the devil," stormed over to Dolores College, and arranged to board there the same day. He was eleven years old.

Despite his arrogant behavior, Fidel became a success at school. His photographic memory helped him do well in his studies. He was a fast runner and excelled in sports, including soccer and basketball. The priests took the boys on field trips in the countryside and encouraged them to hike and climb in the mountains. Fidel earned his teachers' respect because

As a boy, Castro, above, eating a lollipop, *was more interested in sports and hanging out with friends than he was in schoolwork.*

he took on every challenge. The teachers once kept the other students waiting on the bus for hours while Fidel climbed to the top of a peak.

In the summers, Fidel went home to Birán, where he was free to roam the family estate with his brothers and friends. As he grew older, he began to pay attention to the way his father ran the family business. Fidel respected his father, but both of them were proud and stubborn, and they often clashed. Fidel criticized the poor working conditions on the farm. When he was thirteen, he spent his summer vacation trying to convince the sugarcane cutters to band together and demand better treatment from Don Ángel.

HIGH SCHOOL IN HAVANA

After graduating from Dolores College at the age of fifteen, Fidel was admitted to the most prestigious high school in Cuba: Belén College, another all-male Jesuit school. Belén was in Havana, the capital of Cuba, more than five hundred miles from Birán at the opposite end of the island. Lively, sophisticated Havana was nothing like rural Oriente.

The students at Belén came from the most influential families in Cuba. The school's curriculum was demanding, the teachers were well trained, and the students were expected to become leaders. Fidel later explained: "[The Jesuits] valued character, rectitude, honesty, courage and the ability to make sacrifices. . . . The

Jesuits clearly influenced me with their strict organization, their discipline and their values. They contributed to my development and influenced my sense of justice."

Religion played an important role at Belén, as it had at Dolores and La Salle. At all three schools, Fidel had to attend Catholic Mass every day, a requirement he resented. Unlike his mother, he never became very religious, but he was fascinated by the stories in the Bible, especially the ones about battles and wars. Fidel said later that he might have been more interested in religion if his teachers had explained it to him rather than insisting that he believe without understanding why.

Fidel continued to excel in sports—playing baseball, basketball, and soccer and running track. Determined to become the best pitcher on the baseball team, he threw balls against a wall for hours after everyone else had left practice.

Although sports were more important than schoolwork to Fidel, his amazing memory helped him do well on tests. One of his schoolmates recalled that Fidel could recite specific pages from a textbook, complete with punctuation marks. In a speech to university students years later, Fidel noted, "I became a last-minute crammer, which is the worst recommendation you could give to anyone."

Most of Fidel's teachers at Belén were extremely conservative. They believed that Spanish culture was superior to all others and had never forgiven the United States for freeing Cuba from Spanish rule. Fidel's teachers expected him to become a right-wing leader in the Cuban government—someone who would support the interests of wealthy landowners and business owners.

Since Cuban independence in 1902, a series of corrupt leaders had governed the country. Politicians often manipulated elections to win the presidency. In addition, the United States gave financial support to candidates who supported U.S. business interests.

When Fidel entered high school in 1941, Fulgencio Batista y Zaldívar was president of Cuba. Batista, the son of a poor sugarcane cutter, had ruled the country since 1933, when he and a group of his fellow army sergeants overthrew the government after dictator Gerardo Machado was forced to resign. Following the takeover, Batista held the real power in Cuba, even though he wasn't president. He was elected president in 1940 after an honest campaign, but many Cubans grew to hate him because of the corruption in his government. By favoring U.S. businesses that operated in Cuba, Batista became very rich. At the end of his presidential term in 1944, he retired to Florida with 20 million dollars.

Although Fidel showed no interest in politics while he was in high school, he did study the inspiring writings of José Martí, known as the "father of Cuban independence." Martí's poems and essays influenced Fidel's ideas about revolution and social justice.

JOSÉ MARTÍ

José Martí was born in Havana in 1853. At the age of sixteen, he was imprisoned on the Isle of Pines (later renamed the Isle of Youth) for speaking out on behalf of Cuban independence from Spain. After serving six years in prison, he was exiled (forced out of the country) to Spain. In 1881 Martí moved to New York City, where he worked as a reporter for fourteen years.

He dreamed of Cuban independence and of an island in which all citizens would have equal rights and opportunities. Martí expressed his ideals in poetry and prose. In 1892 he met with leading Cuban exiles and convinced them to fight together for democracy. Martí was their chosen leader. In 1895 he was named major general of the Armies of Liberation and secretly landed in Cuba to lead an armed force of six thousand men. A month later, in the rebels' first battle against Spanish troops, Martí was killed when he deliberately rode his horse into the enemy line.

Martí is the most revered hero in Cuban history. Every village and town has a street or major building named after him, and the country's major airport in Havana also bears his name.

In the spring of 1945, Fidel graduated from Belén College near the top of his class. His basketball coach and teacher wrote, "An excellent student and member of the congregation, [Fidel] was an outstanding athlete. . . . He will study law, and we have no doubt he will make a brilliant name for himself."

The seeds of revolution were already being planted in Cuba's youth when Castro enrolled in the University of Havana in 1945.

Chapter **TWO**

FROM LAW TO OUTLAW

CASTRO ENROLLED IN THE UNIVERSITY OF HAVANA'S law school in October 1945. He had no idea what he wanted to do with his life. His six-foot height, powerful build, and piercing brown eyes made an immediate impression, as did his clothing. Most students wore informal, loose cotton shirts, called guayaberas, suitable for the hot and humid weather, but Fidel wore dark pinstripe suits and flashy ties. He persuaded his father to buy him a car, a Ford V-8, to impress the other students. Instead, they thought he was obnoxious and pushy, an outsider with no style.

The political situation in Cuba was tense. Fulgencio Batista, who had been president when Fidel attended Belén College, was living in Florida, but he still kept track of Cuba's politics and its new president, Ramón Grau San Martín. Grau was an extremely popular university professor who had founded the Auténtico Party. He won the 1944 presidential election with Batista's help. Once in office, however, Grau did not carry through with the social reforms he'd promised. Grau and his associates became corrupt, stealing millions of dollars of government funds. The Cubans became angry.

The university in Havana seethed with turmoil. Beatings and shoot-outs were common as armed gangs of students roamed the campus and the city streets. President Grau brought the leaders of the two most powerful rival student gangs, the Socialist Revolutionary Movement (Movimiento Socialista Revolucionaria, or MSR) and the Insurrectional Revolutionary Union (Unión Insurrecional Revolucionaria, or UIR), into his government to make them allies.

POLITICS EQUALS LEADERSHIP

Fidel wanted to become the center of attention. He always preferred to lead rather than follow. The best way to become a leader at the university was to get involved in politics. As the son of a wealthy landowner, Fidel was assumed to be politically conservative, but to the surprise of fellow students, he became a left-wing activist. He saw that Grau's right-wing government was corrupt, favoring the interests of a few rich people while ignoring the struggles of the poor. Although Fidel didn't join any political party, he sided with the student gangs in opposing Grau's government.

Fidel's physical courage during gang fights and fiery, improvised speeches at demonstrations attracted the attention of students—and of the armed, government-supported gangsters who patrolled the campus. Fidel later recalled, "I found myself alone, in open combat with those forces. I had no organization to take them on, no party to support me. It was a rebellion against their attempt to subjugate the university and force-fully impose their will."

Fidel delivered his first official speech at the start of his second year in law school. He attacked President Grau's government and urged the Cuban people to "rise up against those who allowed them to starve to death." The eloquent speech, which he'd rehearsed over and over, was chosen from among many others

A born leader and gifted speaker, Castro inspired his fellow students and angered the Cuban government.

to be quoted in the newspaper. He was beginning to be noticed beyond the university campus.

In 1947 Senator Eduardo (Eddy) Chibás, an immensely popular anti-Grau politician, formed a new political party. The Ortodoxo Party stood for the ideals of José Martí: Cuban independence from Spain, social reforms, and the rights of working people and the poor. Fidel joined the Ortodoxos, even though Eddy Chibás was strongly anti-Communist and Fidel had many Communist friends. The Ortodoxos were much more liberal than Grau's Auténtico Party. They campaigned against poverty, unemployment, low salaries, and political corruption.

POLITICS AND DANGER

Fidel was so focused on political activities that he had no time to attend classes and didn't bother to take exams at the end of his second year at the university. He had no social life, either. Unlike most young Cubans, he didn't hang out at any of the popular nightspots and he didn't dance. He was shy with women. Instead of friends, he had followers and admirers. Instead of chatting, he spoke out against Grau and the violence in Havana. His articles attacking gangs appeared in the student newspaper. Fidel became such a high-profile critic of the government that he was often threatened by the regime's secret police and the MSR, one of the student gangs. These groups tried several times to ambush Fidel, but he always escaped.

When the chief of the secret police finally warned him to leave the university, Fidel realized that he could be killed. But if he acted like a coward, his career as a political leader would be finished. He went to a beach near Havana to think. "Alone, on the beach, facing the sea, I examined the situation," he wrote. "If I returned to the university, I would face personal danger, physical risk. . . . But not to return would be to give in to the threats, to admit my defeat by some killer, to abandon my own ideals and aspirations. I decided to return, and I returned—armed." It was a dangerous decision, but he had to show courage by facing down his enemies. And like them, he carried a pistol.

THE DOMINICAN ADVENTURE

During the summer of 1947, a group of exiles from the Dominican Republic, another island nation east of Cuba, were planning an invasion of their homeland. They had fled to Cuba from the Dominican Republic to escape the oppressive rule of dictator Rafael Trujillo. The exiles wanted to overthrow Trujillo and establish a more democratic government. The Dominicans recruited anyone they could find to join their invasion, including gangsters and students from the university.

Fidel was eager to fight for what he thought was an important cause. Unfortunately, some of his political enemies from the MSR were among the organizers.

THE POLITICAL "ISMS"

uring Fidel Castro's youth, Cuba's political and economic systems were influenced by conflicting views of how a country should be run. These different movements and theories eventually led to tensions between Cuba and other Communist countries and the United States.

Capitalism

Capitalism is an economic system that allows private individuals and companies to own property and make their own business decisions. In a capitalist country such as the United States, private individuals own most of the land, businesses, factories, and other resources and operate them for profit. Although free markets allowing economic competition are important to a capitalist society, the government imposes some rules. These regulations try to prevent monopolies (in which one company controls an entire industry), to shield domestic industries from foreign competition, and to protect the health and safety of workers and consumers. Most capitalist countries have democratic governments.

Socialism

In a socialist country, the government controls most industry. This means that the government decides which products (such as cars) and services (such as medical care) are provided, how they are provided, and how much they cost. Socialism is an economic, not a political, system. One socialist country may be a democracy run by government officials who are elected by the people, while another socialist country might be ruled by a dictator. In most socialist countries, not all industries are controlled by the government. Some are run by private individuals.

Communism

Communism is a political and economic system originally developed by two German philosophers, Karl Marx and Friedrich Engels. They believed that war between ordinary workers and the privileged classes would lead to a society in which all property would be publicly owned. Each person would work and be paid according to his or her needs and abilities. The government, or "state," would control industry. Very few Communist nations remain in the world. In all of them, only one political party exists—the Communist Party. Its leader is the head of the government.

Marxism-Leninism

Marxism-Leninism is the version of Communism developed by Vladimir Lenin, a leader of the 1917 Russian Revolution. Lenin believed in the ideas of Marx and Engels. He helped create a Communist state in Russia, which later became part of the Soviet Union. Lenin set up a dictatorship run by Communist Party officials. The party was supposed to eventually turn over power to the workers, but it remained in control until 1991, when the Soviet Union fell apart.

They refused to accept "that rich kid with pretensions of being a leader." Fidel was afraid he'd be murdered during the invasion, so he persuaded a friend to negotiate a truce with the MSR to ensure his safety.

In late July, he and 1,200 other recruits were shipped to a tiny Cuban island for military training. For two months, the recruits trained and waited under the burning sun while their leaders decided what to do. Finally they set sail, but a few days later, President Grau ordered the Cuban navy to force the boat back to Cuba and arrest everyone on board. As the ship approached Havana, Fidel jumped off and swam eight miles to shore in full uniform. He preferred to take his chances in the shark-infested waters than to stay on the boat, where he might have been killed.

Back at the university, Fidel continued to devote himself to politics, neglecting his studies. As the 1948 presidential elections approached, tensions in Cuba mounted. The government was in turmoil, and the country faced a growing crisis. Havana was becoming a battlefield for pro- and antigovernment forces. President Grau's unconstitutional decision to run for a second term angered students and other Cubans because it was illegal. Fidel called for revolution as the answer. He led demonstrations and accused Grau of betraying the people, saying the peasants still did not have any land and the country's wealth was in foreign hands. Grau's police tried to capture Fidel, but once again he escaped.

REVOLUTION IN COLOMBIA

A new organization for students from Latin American countries was scheduled to meet in Bogotá, Colombia, in April 1948. The organization opposed U.S. influence in Central and South America and supported self-government for all Latin American countries. Fidel agreed to go to Bogotá as a delegate, along with other Cuban students. They represented the younger generation of Cubans, who resented U.S. control of Cuba and supported total independence.

The student meeting was arranged at the same time as an important U.S.-sponsored conference, attended by foreign ministers from many Latin American countries. The students criticized the conference as a U.S. plot to dominate Central and South America. They held demonstrations, heckled the ministers, and tried to disrupt their meetings. One evening Fidel and some others were arrested for distributing leaflets. They were going to be put in prison, but Fidel talked the detectives into letting them go.

The political situation in Colombia exploded a few days later when Jorge Eliécer Gaitán, a hero of the Liberal Party, was assassinated. For more than two years, Colombians had been caught up in a civil war between the rival Conservative (right-wing) and Liberal (left-wing) parties. Thousands of people had been killed. Colombians' anger and grief over Gaitán's death erupted in rioting, looting, and gunfire that lasted for days.

After Jorge Gaitán's assassination, thousands of supporters gathered for a memorial rally in Bogotá, Colombia.

First, Fidel watched, then he joined in. "I realized that it was a revolution, so I decided to be part of it as one more person. . . . I knew that the people were oppressed and were right to rebel; I also knew that Gaitán's death was a terrible crime," he said. Fidel joined a vast river of people armed with everything from sticks to rifles. He was wearing a suit and dress shoes, but when he found a pair of boots, a beret, and a police officer's jacket, he quickly put them on. He was ready for combat.

"I joined the crowd who said they were going somewhere—but nobody knew where," he wrote. "There was tremendous disorder, almost no discipline, and no organization." This was no way to run a revolution, he decided.

On April 11, the Conservative government and the Liberal opposition reached an agreement, finally ending

Colombia's civil war. Two days later, the Cuban students were flown home to Havana. Their arrival made the front pages of the Havana newspapers. Fidel was right where he liked to be—in the limelight.

Presidential elections in Cuba were planned for June 1, 1948. Fidel supported the Ortodoxo Party candidate, Eddy Chibás. He and Chibás spent many weeks campaigning together in Oriente Province. The Ortodoxos were honest in their dealings and refused to make bargains with other parties. But the Auténticos made deals, bought votes, and spent huge sums to support their new candidate, Carlos Prío Socarrás. Prío won the election. Chibás, despite his popularity, placed next to last, just ahead of the Communist candidate. The new president's administration soon proved to be even more corrupt than Grau's.

POLITICS AND MARRIAGE

Fidel returned to law school in September 1948. In October he married Mirta Díaz-Balart, a philosophy student at the university whom he'd known for many years. Mirta was also from Oriente Province. Her wealthy family had strong ties to former president Batista, and they disliked the politics of their new son-in-law. The Castros, however, were delighted by the Díaz-Balarts' political connections. Ángel Castro paid for a big wedding and a long honeymoon in the United States. Batista even gave Fidel and Mirta two five-hundred-dollar bills for a gift.

Castro and Mirta pose on a beach in Puerto Rico a few months before their marriage.

Despite Fidel's negative stance toward the United States, he and Mirta spent several weeks in New York. They rented an apartment in the Bronx, and Fidel took classes to improve his English. For the first time in many years, he felt safe. But he wanted to finish law school, so he and Mirta returned to Cuba. A year later, on September 1, 1949, the couple had a son, Félix Fidel Castro Díaz-Balart, nicknamed Fidelito. Fidel adored the baby, but politics consumed his time and energy. The marriage suffered as a result.

During Fidel's fourth year of law school, he thought about running for Cuba's congress in the next election. To build his reputation, he reached out to the neglected poor districts of Havana. He talked with people on the streets, visited them at home and work, and broadcast a weekly radio address. He campaigned against "injustice, poverty, unemployment, high rents, low salaries, and political corruption." At a large meeting on campus, he denounced the gangs and their leaders. As he finished talking, cars with armed gangsters determined to kill him began to surround the university. But friends helped Fidel sneak away, and they hid him for two weeks. He decided to return to New York until tempers cooled. Mirta and Fidelito stayed home.

Fidel returned to Cuba in early 1950. This time he was determined to graduate from law school. He devoted the next several months to his studies. Relying on his incredible memory, he learned two years' worth of course work in six months. Finally, in September 1950, Fidel graduated and was qualified to practice law. Mirta's family could have helped him get a highly paid job, but he didn't care about money. Although his family still sent him an allowance, his friends noted that "Fidel often gave it away the moment it arrived."

He decided to work for the poor instead and formed a partnership with two other Havana law school graduates. Peasants, students, and workers knew they could turn to the Azpiazo, Castro & Resende firm to solve their legal problems. But in their three years together, the lawyers earned very little money, because Fidel insisted that they work for free. The partnership broke up when Fidel left to take the first step toward revolution.

Castro, standing, center, *poses with fellow rebels during preparation for the Moncada army barracks attack.*

Chapter **THREE**

REBEL WITH A CAUSE

ON AUGUST 5, 1951, EDDY CHIBÁS, LEADER OF the Ortodoxo Party, shocked the country by shooting himself during the broadcast of his weekly radio program. For a month, Cubans had listened eagerly as Chibás accused President Prío's education minister of a vast corruption scheme. Chibás had promised to prove his allegations during the August 5 broadcast, but he couldn't do so, because the politicians who held the evidence decided not to give him the documents. He hoped that by publicly shooting himself, he would rouse the Cuban people to action. Chibás died of his gunshot wounds eleven days later.

Despite the loss of his mentor, Fidel decided to run in the congressional elections of 1952. The other

Ortodoxo Party leaders didn't support him, but he convinced citizens in two Havana districts to nominate him as their Ortodoxo candidate. Fidel campaigned hard, spreading his message on the radio, in mass mailings, and in fiery speeches. His growing reputation for speaking the truth and fighting government corruption drew large crowds. Everyone assumed that he would win a seat in the Chamber of Deputies.

A STOLEN ELECTION

Fidel's hard work came to nothing, because the election was never held. General Batista had returned from Florida, determined to become president of Cuba again. Realizing that he would lose in a fair election, Batista seized power illegally, overthrowing the government of President Carlos Prío. Batista proclaimed himself chief of state on March 10, 1952, beginning his dictatorship.

Most Cubans hated Batista for crushing democracy, but U.S. leaders decided to recognize his government as legitimate. They believed that he would protect U.S. business investments in Cuba and oppose the Communists. Although the Cuban Communist Party was weak, many people in the United States feared that the Soviet Union had organized a Communist plot to dominate the world. A popular theory at the time was that one country after another would "fall" like dominoes to Communism.

Fidel decided that the only answer to Cuba's problems was to lead a movement to overthrow the dictator and restore democracy to the country. He never doubted that he would succeed, and his supreme self-confidence, courage, and organizational skills drew others to his cause. Immediately after Batista took over, Fidel went into hiding. For the next fifteen months, he moved frequently among the houses of trusted friends. He wrote articles opposing Batista and calling on Cubans to remove him by force. Since Batista controlled the press, Fidel could not publish his articles in the major newspapers. He asked a friend who owned a mimeograph machine for help. (A mimeograph is a hand-cranked copy machine that was used before photocopiers were invented.) His supporters made hundreds of copies of the articles and distributed them in the streets. Fidel also brought a lawsuit against Batista for violating the constitution. Although newspapers weren't allowed to publish Fidel's articles, they did report on his antigovernment activities.

A small group of supporters formed the core of Fidel's revolutionary movement. They included his brother Raúl; an accountant named Abel Santamaría and his sister Haydée; and Melba Hernández, an Ortodoxo lawyer. Two other women played important roles. Fidel's half-sister Lidia let him use her apartment while he was on the run. Natalia "Naty" Revuelta, the beautiful wife of a Havana heart surgeon, offered her apartment as a hideout, gave money to the rebel cause, and became Fidel's mistress. The only woman in Fidel's life who wasn't involved in his plans was his wife, Mirta. He rarely saw her and left her and his young son in their Havana apartment without money for food or shelter. He assumed that either his family or hers would take care of them.

A FAILED ATTACK

Fidel devised a daring and risky plan to capture the Moncada army barracks in downtown Santiago de Cuba. Moncada was the second largest military compound in Cuba, home to one thousand trained soldiers. Fidel assumed that once his small rebel force mounted a surprise attack on the fort, many of the soldiers would join their cause. He planned to use the fort's radio transmitter to broadcast an appeal to the Cuban people to rise up against Batista. He also intended to seize the weapons and ammunition at Moncada.

Fidel recruited about 150 men and women willing to fight against the Batista government. He organized his recruits into small units and demanded their total loyalty. To keep his plans from being discovered by Batista's secret police, he controlled all the details. He and his core advisers spent several months preparing the attack and raising money for food, ammunition, and weapons. Pedro Miret, one of Fidel's military commanders, owned an ancient submachine gun, but the other rebels had to settle for sports rifles and hunting guns. Fidel wasn't concerned about their inferior weapons because he planned to take Moncada by surprise with a minimum of force and no bloodshed.

The rebels bought a small farm outside Santiago to use as a base of operations. Fidel chose July 26, 1953, as the day for the attack. At five o'clock that morning, he and 125 followers left the farmhouse in a convoy of automobiles to begin their assault.

From the moment they drove away, everything that could have gone wrong did. One car got a flat tire, and two others got lost. By the time the rebels reached their destination, only 111 fighters remained, including Fidel. The trip had taken too long, and dawn broke just as the attack began. The rebels lost their chance to surprise the guards in the darkness. Soldiers began firing on them with submachine guns, and Fidel ordered a retreat after less than half an hour. Eight rebels were killed in the short battle.

Batista's forces were already in place for a counterattack when Castro and his rebels arrived at the Moncada barracks on July 26, 1953.

The survivors broke into small groups to try to escape from the army. Fidel hid out in the nearby Gran Piedra Mountains with about twenty of his men. Within a week, sixty-one more rebels were killed. The rest, including Fidel and Raúl Castro, were captured and held in the Santiago jail. The uprising had been a spectacular failure.

THE TRIAL OF THE REBELS

As they awaited trial, the jailed rebels stayed in constant communication with each other. Although Fidel was kept in solitary confinement, the others passed secret messages to him, sometimes with the cooperation of friendly guards. Fidel decided that only his well-known supporters should plead guilty to the charges. Many of the others were completely unknown to the authorities, and since the government couldn't prove their involvement, they could deny participating in the uprising. The captured rebels agreed to the plan, and only twenty-nine of them pleaded guilty.

Beginning on September 21, 1953, the government attempted to try Fidel and the other defendants at the Santiago Palace of Justice. The prisoners were led in wearing handcuffs, but Fidel protested, and the judge ordered the cuffs removed. Fidel proudly admitted his part in the uprising and demanded to act as his own lawyer. He had to borrow a black robe, the traditional attire for Cuban lawyers appearing in court. Using his spellbinding skills as an orator, Fidel turned the tables

on the prosecution (the prosecutor is a lawyer represent-
ing the government), putting Batista on trial for crushing
democracy in Cuba. The few journalists who were
allowed into the courtroom were prevented from publishing their reports, but news about Fidel reached the
streets anyway.

After five days of bad publicity, government officials
decided to keep Fidel out of the courtroom. They
claimed that he needed to be hospitalized. Fidel was
afraid he would be secretly murdered and the government would say he'd died from an illness. He smug-
gled a letter to Melba, one of the rebel prisoners,
stating that he was healthy. She sneaked it into court
under a head scarf and dramatically handed it to the
chief judge. The letter may have saved Fidel's life.

While the government waited to try Fidel, the trial
of the remaining rebels continued. All twenty-nine
were convicted. Raúl Castro and the other top leaders
were sentenced to thirteen years in prison, but Melba
Hernández and Haydée Santamaría had to serve just
seven months in a women's prison near Havana.

"HISTORY WILL ABSOLVE ME"

The government stuck by its official story that Fidel
was too ill to return to the Palace of Justice and
arranged to try him secretly in a Santiago hospital. At
9:00 A.M. on October 16, 1953, military guards led
Fidel into a tiny basement room. About forty people
were present, including three judges, the prosecutor,

and six journalists. Despite the heat and humidity in the airless hospital room, Fidel wore a heavy, dark blue wool suit, white shirt, and tie. After more than two months in prison, he was so thin that his watch dangled on his wrist.

The prosecutor took only two minutes to make the case against Fidel and asked the court to hand down the maximum sentence—twenty-six years in prison. Fidel was allowed to act as his own lawyer. Once again, his handcuffs were removed and he had to borrow a black robe. The robe, much too small for him, split at the seams when he raised his arm to make a point.

Fidel delivered a passionate, two-hour speech defending his actions. He admitted that he had planned to overthrow the government. Then he accused the Batista regime of illegally seizing power and stealing money that should have been spent to improve the lives of poor Cubans. He compared the honorable way his men had treated the soldiers they captured with the brutal behavior of army officers who had tortured and murdered captured rebels. Using examples from history, including the opening words of the American Declaration of Independence, Fidel defended the right of a people to rebel against an unjust government.

Throughout his speech, he quoted from the writings of José Martí. Fidel ended by declaring, "But I do not fear prison, as I do not fear the fury of the miserable tyrant who took the lives of seventy of my comrades. Condemn me. It does not matter. History will absolve [free] me."

PRISON ON THE ISLE OF PINES

The chief judge sentenced the twenty-seven-year-old rebel leader to fifteen years in prison. Surrounded by armed guards, Fidel walked out of the hospital to the cheers of people in the street. Along with Raúl and the other men, Fidel was sent to prison on the Isle of Pines, fifty miles south of Havana in the Caribbean Sea.

The rebels were all housed together. They started a library and organized a prison "university." For five hours a day, they studied philosophy, world history, economics, mathematics, Spanish literature, and foreign languages. Fidel's personal reading list included everything from popular novels to *Das Kapital*, the original description of Communist theory by Karl Marx. In a letter to a friend, Fidel wrote, "What a formidable school this prison is . . . from here, I can finish forging my vision of the world and the sense of my life."

Even in prison, Fidel defied Batista. When Batista visited the Isle of Pines in February 1954, Fidel made sure the general heard the men singing the "July 26th March," a revolutionary anthem composed by one of the rebels in honor of the Moncada attack. Batista left in a rage, and the prison commander placed Fidel in solitary confinement for the next fourteen months. Fidel continued to read and to write letters to his

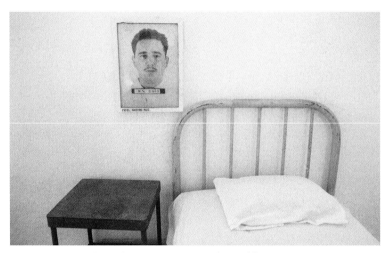

Castro served less than two years of his fifteen-year sentence in this jail cell.

family and friends. Many of his letters were to Naty Revuelta, who supplied him with books. Fidel suggested that she read the books too, so that they could discuss them in their letters to each other.

After Melba Hernández and Haydée Santamaría were released from the women's prison, Fidel found ways to get messages to them and other friends, even though the prison guards censored his mail. Sometimes he wrote in tiny handwriting on small pieces of paper that he hid in matchboxes or cigars and gave to visitors to smuggle out. Other times he used lemon juice to write invisible messages between the lines in letters. The letters passed inspection at the prison, but when the recipients heated them, the secret messages appeared.

Fidel spent months re-creating the speech he'd given in court and smuggling it out in tiny sections. He urged Melba, Haydée, and Lidia to mass-produce the document and distribute at least 100,000 copies. Reassembling the fifty-four-page speech, typing it, and getting it printed was an enormous task, but the women succeeded in producing 27,500 copies. The "History Will Absolve Me" speech became one of the most famous documents of the revolution.

While in prison, Fidel rarely wrote to Mirta and saw her and Fidelito only a few times. But he assumed that she was loyal to him. He was shocked when she demanded a divorce in July 1954. She then left for the United States with Fidelito. Fidel agreed to the divorce but fought to regain custody of his five-year-old son.

On November 1, 1954, Batista was elected president of Cuba, after ensuring that he was the only candidate running. Six months later, the government announced a general amnesty (pardon) for political prisoners. All the rebels, including Fidel, were released.

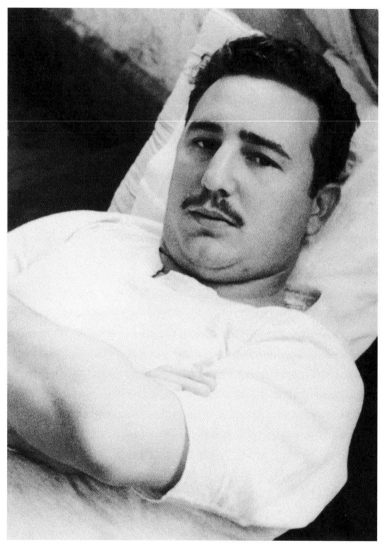

Fearing for his life after his release from prison, Castro fled to Mexico, where this photo was taken.

Chapter **FOUR**

THE PATH TO POWER

THE PEOPLE OF HAVANA TREATED FIDEL LIKE A HERO when he returned from the Isle of Pines. Once again, he publicly challenged Batista, but the government banned Fidel from speaking on the radio and shut down newspapers that printed his articles. Fidel knew that his life was in danger, and he decided that he had to leave Cuba right away. He and his brother Raúl went to Mexico to prepare for a revolution. Pedro Miret, a loyal ally from the Moncada defeat, and Frank País, a military strategist, stayed in Cuba to recruit fighters for the cause. They would send only the best to Mexico to become part of Fidel's Rebel Army.

When Fidel was in prison, he had had a lot of time to plan an attack on Batista's government. First, he had to organize and train an army. He chose Mexico as the training site because it was close, safe, and home to many exiles from Cuba and other Latin American countries. After their training, the troops would travel by boat to Cuba, hide out in the Sierra Maestra—a rugged, forested mountain range—and fight a guerrilla war from there. (In guerrilla warfare, small, independent groups fight large, organized armies. The guerrillas usually hide in mountains, forests, or rugged country and ambush or harass the army.) Fidel's goal was to overthrow Batista and then establish a new government.

TRAINING GUERRILLAS

Fidel established headquarters in Mexico City for his revolutionary effort, which was called the July 26th Movement in memory of the attack on the Moncada barracks. He worked around the clock persuading Cuban refugees, exiles from other Latin American countries, and rich, well-connected Mexicans to give money and support to the movement. Fidel convinced General Alberto Bayo, an expert in guerrilla warfare, to train the Rebel Army.

The group's leadership in Cuba, including Miret, País, and a woman named Celia Sánchez, kept Fidel informed of the events there. Celia Sánchez had been involved in politics for many years. Dedicated to the ideals of the July 26th Movement, she became one of its leaders in Cuba. She wanted to join the invasion force training in Mexico but was persuaded to organize a secret network of peasant supporters in the Sierra Maestra instead.

Fidel met another key supporter, Ernesto "Che" Guevara, in Mexico City in August 1955. Che was working as a doctor, but the pay was so low that he had to take a second job as a news photographer. He had heard about Fidel through the "revolutionary grapevine" and from some Fidelistas—the nickname for Fidel's followers—whom he'd met in Guatemala. The two men spoke together for hours as soon as they were introduced. Che noted, "Within a few hours of our meeting, in the early morning, I had already become one of his future revolutionaries."

The two men were intellectual equals, and they spent long hours in intense discussions about how to

Ernesto "Che" Guevara, right, *and Castro became instant friends and fellow revolutionaries. They shared many of the same goals and beliefs.*

fix the world. Che believed in Fidel's ideals and leadership. He quickly became a trusted member of Fidel's inner circle.

Fidel had learned from the Moncada attack that he couldn't expect to topple Batista's government overnight. The revolution would take time and money.

CHE GUEVARA

Ernesto "Che" Guevara was a young Argentine doctor who preferred revolution to medicine. A Marxist-Leninist, he believed that the United States had too much control over the economic and political affairs of South and Central America. After graduating from medical school, Guevara traveled throughout Latin America. The widespread poverty he saw strengthened his hatred of the United States.

Guevara joined Fidel's rebels as a doctor but became a fighter. The Cubans nicknamed him Che, an Argentine expression akin to "Hey," which Guevara used frequently. Like Fidel, Che was daring, brilliant, and a hard worker. Before long he became Fidel's top commander.

After the revolution, Che became Cuba's minister of finance and minister of industry. Young radicals all over the world idolized him and his ideals. But Che's main ambition was to spread revolution to other Latin American countries. In 1965 he went to Bolivia, hoping to organize the peasants against the government. Two years later, he was captured by the Bolivian military, with the help of the U.S. Central Intelligence Agency (CIA), and executed. Posters bearing Che's image are seen everywhere in Cuba, and he has become a legend throughout the world.

He decided, like José Martí before him, to seek support and funds in the United States. For seven weeks, Fidel traveled along the East Coast, speaking to thousands of Cuban exiles, especially in New York City and Miami, Florida. He declared that the invasion of Cuba would take place the following year: "I can inform you with complete reliability that in 1956, we will be free or we will be martyrs!"

Fidel's sister Lidia brought Fidelito to Miami. It was the first time Fidel had seen his son since the divorce. Lidia also brought Fidelito to Mexico, where Fidel saw him as often as possible.

Fidel's appearances were not reported by the U.S. press, but his fund-raising was a success. He had enough money to buy weapons and set up training for sixty guerrillas. Extra money went for food and housing. The men trained to endure the harshest conditions—they had to be able to walk day and night in terrible weather, eat and drink very little for days, and sleep on the ground. To get in shape, they marched for hours every day, hiked in the mountains carrying heavy backpacks, and practiced shooting.

Back in Cuba, most Cubans were fed up with the government. Batista didn't care that the majority of citizens were poor and illiterate. He just wanted to get rich. Attacks on Batista's regime by students and workers were more frequent and better organized, but none succeeded. Hundreds of dissenters were thrown into prison or killed.

News about Fidel's movement was spreading to other countries. Supporters sent money that Fidel used to buy better weapons. In the summer of 1956, the rebels moved to Mexico's southeastern coast to launch the invasion.

RETURN TO CUBA

Fidel found a leaky, secondhand yacht, called the *Granma,* anchored on a Mexican river. He bought the boat because the price was reasonable. He insisted that the *Granma* could carry his rebel group to Cuba, even though it could hold only twenty-five people and needed many repairs. The boat had to be fixed quickly so the invasion could take place before the year's end. Even the news that Fidel's father had died in Birán on October 21 didn't slow the pace of his preparations to leave Mexico.

Early on the morning of November 25, Fidel and eighty-one rebels sailed for Cuba on a stormy sea. The trip was a nightmare—the weather was terrible, everyone was seasick, an engine broke down, seawater leaked in, and fresh water and food ran out. Progress was slow, since the yacht was overloaded with eighty-two heavily armed passengers. Fidel had told the rebel leaders in Cuba to expect the *Granma* to land at a prearranged spot on the Oriente coast on November 30, but the voyage took seven days instead of five.

Miret, País, Sánchez, and the other rebels in Cuba didn't know about the delay. When the *Granma* didn't appear on November 30, they pulled back their forces. On a moonless night two days later, as the *Granma* neared Cuba, the captain realized they were lost. As dawn broke, the boat hit a mud bank just off the coast, far from the planned landing site. Fidel, Che, and the other men were stuck in a dangerous swamp. They had to carry their weapons ashore, wading through mud, huge tree roots, and clouds of mosquitoes. It took two hours for them to reach firm ground. They lost their food and most of the supplies.

Batista had been alerted that his enemy had landed in Oriente. Forty thousand government soldiers, armed with new weapons, tanks, and jet planes supplied by the United States, awaited Fidel's eighty-one men. As soon as the rebels landed, they were spotted by a naval patrol boat, and a group of Batista's soldiers was sent to search for the men. But they failed to find them. Fidel and his troops walked east toward the Sierra Maestra, where they could hide in the region's isolated forests, steep valleys, and rock-covered hills.

THE REVOLUTION

On December 5, 1956, after three days of marching, the exhausted men set up camp on a low hill. Suddenly, gunfire broke out all around them. They were caught in an ambush, surrounded by Batista's heavily armed rural police guard. Fidel yelled commands, trying to keep his troops organized in the midst of the gunfire, but it was impossible. Finally, several men dragged him away from the battlefield. He and two others escaped together. "There was a moment when I was Commander in Chief of myself and two others," Fidel said. The rebel force was destroyed. Of eighty-two soldiers, only a few remained.

With most of the rebels dead or captured, Batista assumed that Fidel had been among those killed. The general ordered his troops to withdraw from the mountains. Fidel's friends and relatives also thought that he was dead. But he was hiding in the mountains, guided,

Castro, seated, *set up base for his Rebel Army in the Sierra Maestra.*

fed, and protected by the network of peasants Celia had organized. Eventually, Fidel, Raúl, and Che were reunited. The entire Rebel Army consisted of sixteen survivors with twelve weapons, backed by the tough peasants, or *guajiros,* who were devoted to the cause.

The guajiros were poor, illiterate people who lived in villages and farms in the Sierra Maestra. Che helped them build farms, a small hospital, and a cigar factory. He also started a newspaper and radio station. In return, the peasants gave the rebels protection and support. The guajiro network informed the rebels if government troops or other strangers were in the area.

VICTORY

Reports about Fidel's July 26th Movement reached the United States, where the news coverage was favorable. New recruits joined the guerrillas. While the Rebel Army fought in the mountains, other Fidelistas took action in the cities and countryside. July 26th members destroyed sugarcane fields, police stations, army barracks, and supply lines. Meanwhile, student violence—bombings, strikes, and assassinations—maddened Batista's forces. Their response was so brutal that most Cubans turned against Batista. And the United States decided to withdraw its support for him.

By the summer of 1958, Fidel had united all the anti-Batista groups under his leadership. Batista made one last effort to wipe out Fidel's troops. He launched an all-out air and ground attack, sending ten thousand soldiers to the Sierra Maestra. After seventy-six days of fierce fighting, the Rebel Army conquered the government forces. Radio broadcasts from Fidel's secret headquarters announced their victory.

Batista's government was close to collapse. His army suffered defeat after defeat. As rebel units led by Che Guevara and Camilo Cienfuegos—another heroic commander—advanced westward toward Havana, government soldiers left their posts and joined them. Guevara led the attack that captured the town of Santa Clara on December 28 and finally toppled the Batista government.

Shortly after midnight on January 1, 1959, Batista fled to the Dominican Republic. Fidel ordered Guevara, Cienfuegos, and their troops to march to Havana. Along the way, they seized the major army posts. On January 2, Guevara and Cienfuegos entered Havana while Fidel took Santiago. The next day, his troops began a five-day victory march down the central highway toward Havana. Sitting atop a tank, wearing olive green fatigues, and carrying his favorite semiautomatic rifle, Fidel addressed the cheering crowds along the way. As he neared Havana, he was reunited with nine-year-old Fidelito for the first time since they'd parted in Mexico two years before. (Soon after, Mirta and her second husband left to live in Spain, and Fidel took custody of his son.)

All over Cuba, revolutionary troops took possession of government buildings and police and radio stations.

Castro triumphantly returned to Havana atop a military jeep, flanked by soldiers from his Rebel Army and many supporters.

The takeover was surprisingly calm. Officials and police from Batista's regime were captured and jailed, while people imprisoned by Batista for political crimes were set free.

Fidel entered Havana on January 8. That night thousands gathered to hear his victory speech. "We cannot become dictators," he declared. "We shall never need to use force because we have the people . . . and because the day the people want, I shall leave." Fidel had achieved his ultimate goal.

Castro and his Rebel Army are pictured on this poster for the Cuban Revolution.

Chapter **FIVE**

CUBA IN TRANSITION

IN THE WEEKS FOLLOWING THE "PEOPLE'S REVOLU-
tion," as Fidel called it, he appointed a respected former
judge, Manuel Urrutia, as Cuba's president and promised
to allow democratic elections within two years. Urrutia
chose a group of political moderates from the July 26th
Movement to serve as his ministers, but Fidel was still
firmly in charge. He remained commander in chief of
the army and was referred to as the "Maximum Leader"
by an adoring Cuban public. Fidel had two goals: to rid
Cuba of U.S. influence and to completely remake the
country's economy and social structure.

MISLEADING THE UNITED STATES
To carry out his plan to transform Cuban society,

Castro relied heavily on his inner circle of advisers. From left to right: *Celia Sánchez, Raúl Castro, and Che Guevara.*

Fidel organized a hidden government that included his most trusted advisers, Raúl, Che, and Celia. They shared Fidel's commitment to creating a socialist state in which the government, rather than individual citizens, would own businesses, set the prices of goods, and determine the wages paid to workers. Citizens would work for the public good rather than their own profit. While the official government met in the presidential palace, Fidel's secret team met in his penthouse at the Havana Hilton Hotel to plan radical reforms of agriculture, banking, and industry.

Fidel soon forced the president to appoint him prime minister. He also had the constitution changed so that he would control government policy. From then on, the president's only job was to sign laws proposed by the prime minister, Fidel.

Although Fidel never joined the Communist Party, he gradually became convinced that Communism was the right choice for Cuba. At the University of Havana,

Fidel had had many friends who were Communists, but he felt that the party was weak and could not give him the backing he needed. Later, under Che Guevara's influence, Fidel developed his own version of Communism to carry out his plans for radical change. He created special "revolutionary instruction schools," which claimed to be teaching young Fidelistas how to govern a democracy. The schools' real purpose, however, was to educate youth about the ideas of Marx and Lenin. Only one political party would be allowed in the new Cuba—the Communist Party.

Fidel had not yet publicly revealed his true plans for Cuba, but the U.S. government didn't trust him to support U.S. interests. Officially the U.S. government appeared friendly, but by March 1959, the CIA began plotting secretly to overthrow the Cuban leader. A month later, Fidel was invited to speak at a meeting of newspaper editors in Washington, D.C. During the visit, he denied being a Communist and insisted that

During his visit to the United States in 1959, Castro was amused to find this headline in a local paper.

Cuba was a democracy. But in a television interview, he ruled out elections, saying, "Real democracy is not possible for a hungry people."

FIDEL TAKES CONTROL

When Fidel returned to Havana, he drew up a radical land reform law, which was quickly approved. It limited the amount of land individual Cubans could own and allowed the government to seize the rest without paying the owners. The new law was very popular with the peasants, most of whom owned little or no land. The law also created the National Institute for Agrarian Reform, which merged with the Rebel Army to become Fidel's power base. He replaced the moderate government ministers with trusted revolutionaries. Then he forced President Urrutia to resign and put a Fidelista in his place. Raúl took over the armed forces, and Che was put in charge of industry and banking.

Fidel claimed that he had to control the media to protect the revolution from its enemies. Only two newspapers were allowed to remain in print—one run by the July 26th Movement and the other by the Cuban Communist Party. Both papers published only articles approved by Fidel. Criticism of the Maximum Leader wasn't allowed. The government also took over the two main television stations and all the radio stations. Within a year, freedom of the press had disappeared in Cuba.

Cuban citizens were expected to join groups called Committees for the Defense of the Revolution. Committee members patrolled their neighborhoods looking for illegal behavior, suspicious people, and antigovernment activities. They reported their findings to the security service and the police. The information gathered was used to arrest thousands of Cubans as "enemies of the revolution." Many of them were executed, including some people who had helped Fidel overthrow Batista but later disagreed with his plan to turn Cuba into a Communist state.

In the years after Fidel came to power, thousands of Cubans fled into exile. The first to leave were Batista supporters, gangsters, and anti-Communist politicians. But many middle- and upper-class Cubans also left when Fidel's economic reforms drastically lowered their standard of living. By 1963 there were 250,000 exiles, including doctors, teachers, engineers, technicians, and businesspeople. Most of the exiles settled in Miami, Florida.

Once Fidel eliminated political opposition and silenced the independent press, he began to introduce social reforms. He called on all Cubans to work hard for the common good rather than their personal gain. Since nearly half the population was unable to read or write, Fidel started a crash program to train more teachers. New government programs also educated doctors, set up a public health system, built decent housing for workers, and improved roads in rural areas. Living conditions for peasants and workers improved greatly, increasing Fidel's popularity among the poor.

Fidel's efforts to restructure the economy were much less successful. He believed that Cuba shouldn't depend so heavily on sugar sales to bring in cash. His plan to cut back on sugar production and build factories to manufacture other goods was a disaster. So he reversed his position and forced most Cuban workers to concentrate on producing a record amount of sugar. That plan failed too. Fidel had creative ideas for new businesses, but none of them worked. He and his advisers had no understanding of business, and most of the experienced professionals had left the country.

A New Ally

Two of Fidel's priorities were to modernize his army and create a new militia—a civilian military force that could assist the regular army in an emergency. In early 1959, he was able to purchase weapons from the United States and its allies. Within a few months, however, U.S. leaders had begun to feel uneasy about Fidel's intentions. The United States banned arms sales to Cuba and pressured the Europeans to do the same. Fidel then turned to the Soviet Union. The Soviets realized that Cuba's location near the United States was important to their political and military strategy.

After World War II, a rivalry known as the Cold War had developed between the United States and the Soviet Union, the world's two superpowers. Each nation formed military and economic alliances with as many other countries as possible. They fought using words and economic and political actions. Both sides avoided using weapons, since each had nuclear arms and was afraid of starting a war that would destroy both countries and cause a worldwide environmental disaster.

In February 1960, Cuba and the Soviet Union established diplomatic relations and signed their first trade agreement. The Soviets agreed to buy one million tons of Cuban sugar each year, loan the Cuban government 100 million dollars, and sell weapons, raw materials, and manufactured goods to Cuba.

As Cuba's ties to the Soviet Union grew stronger, its relationship with the United States deteriorated. In June 1960, the Cuban government took over all U.S.-owned oil refineries. In return, the United States stopped buying Cuban sugar. This was a huge loss to the Cuban economy, since the United States provided the largest source of trade income to Cuba. Fidel retaliated by seizing all U.S. property within his country, worth almost one billion dollars. Then U.S. president Dwight D. Eisenhower banned most exports to Cuba. This prompted Nikita Khrushchev, the Soviet premier, to remark, "Castro will have to gravitate to us like an iron filing to a magnet."

During his dispute with the United States, Fidel returned to New York to attend the twenty-fifth anniversary session of the United Nations (UN). As usual, he made headlines. He stormed out of his hotel, complaining that the room prices were too high. Wearing army fatigues and trailed by fifty Cuban delegates and hundreds of reporters, Fidel marched into the office of the top UN official. He declared that he and his men would sleep in the UN building or outside in the park. In the middle of the night, the Cubans moved into the Theresa Hotel in Harlem, a mostly black neighborhood.

While in New York, Fidel met Soviet premier Khrushchev for the first time. Standing in front of the hotel, they made an odd-looking pair—the tall, bearded Cuban bending down to embrace the short, plump, bald Russian.

THE UNITED STATES TARGETS FIDEL

The U.S. government became openly hostile to Fidel as a result of his anti-American speeches, his takeover of U.S. businesses in Cuba, and his new, close relationship with the Soviet Union. During the 1960s, the CIA made many attempts to kill or embarrass the Cuban leader. Although U.S. presidents approved the policy of eliminating Fidel, they were careful to avoid learning the details of the plots. CIA officials planned and carried out the covert (secret) operations, so the U.S. president could deny involvement if necessary.

Many of the plots against Fidel were so fantastic that they could have come from a spy novel: putting

Fidel Castro, left, *meets with Nikita Khrushchev,* right, *in New York. Because of Cuba's proximity to the United States, an enemy of the Soviet Union, Castro was a valuable ally for Khrushchev.*

poison in gift boxes of his favorite cigars, sprinkling a chemical in his shoes that would make his beard fall out, contaminating the radio station where he broadcast his speeches with a spray that would cause him to hallucinate, placing a beautiful seashell filled with explosives where he often went diving, and giving him a diving suit dusted with a fungus that would cause a skin disease. The CIA also offered the Mafia $150,000 to assassinate Fidel.

None of the schemes to kill Fidel succeeded. But the CIA also had another strategy. The agency began recruiting and training anti-Castro exiles to invade Cuba and take over Fidel's government.

Castro leaps from a tank as he arrives at the Bay of Pigs. The failed invasion was a publicity coup for the Cuban leader.

Chapter **SIX**

THE UNITED STATES VS. CUBA

JOHN F. KENNEDY BECAME PRESIDENT OF THE UNITED
States on January 20, 1961, just three weeks after President Eisenhower cut diplomatic ties with Cuba. Kennedy
promised 25 billion dollars in aid to other Latin American countries if they did the same. All but Mexico agreed.

Kennedy also inherited Eisenhower's plans to invade
Cuba. Kennedy agreed that the United States should
plan and finance an invasion, but he insisted that no
U.S. citizens take part in the fighting. He didn't want
other countries to think the United States was a big
bully picking on a much smaller, weaker nation.

THE BAY OF PIGS

CIA plans called for a surprise attack by Cuban exiles,

who would land on the beaches of the Bay of Pigs, on the southern coast of Cuba. The exiles would set up a secure base camp, establish a temporary government there, and request international recognition for the new government. Then they would join forces with anti-Castro guerrillas in the nearby mountains and cut off the three highways leading to the rest of Cuba. U.S. ships anchored in the bay would deliver supplies.

Before the invasion could begin, Fidel's air force had to be destroyed. On April 15, 1961, eight U.S. Air Force bombers, painted to look like Cuban planes and flown by CIA-trained pilots, attacked Cuba's three air force bases. The bomber pilots thought they'd destroyed all of Cuba's warplanes, but most of the damaged planes were actually civilian jets. Five warplanes were destroyed, but eight remained in fighting condition.

The CIA didn't know that Fidel's spies had informed him of the planned invasion, though they weren't sure exactly where or when it would occur. The attack on Cuba's air force alerted Fidel that an invasion was looming. Since he had often vacationed at the Bay of Pigs, he was aware that the beaches there would make a good place for invading forces to land.

On April 16, Kennedy ordered the invasion to begin. At one o'clock the next morning, when 1,500 fighters landed at the Bay of Pigs, more than 1,000 armed Cuban troops with tanks were waiting. Fidel had another surprise: his remaining warplanes destroyed two of the U.S. ships carrying ammunition and supplies.

The other U.S. ships turned around and headed out of the bay, leaving the invaders stranded.

Although the exile forces fought hard, they could not gain control of the beaches or the highways. Contrary to CIA expectations, Cubans united to defend the revolution against their enemy. In addition, the anti-Castro guerrillas had been arrested before the invasion, so they could not help. With victory near, Fidel left his secret headquarters in Havana and traveled to the battle site to encourage his troops. He also took advantage of the publicity—a photo of him jumping off a tank onto the beach was made into millions of posters.

Within two days, the last of the invaders surrendered. Nearly 1,200 exiles were imprisoned in Havana. More

Only fourteen of the exiles, above, *who took part in the Bay of Pigs invasion escaped death or imprisonment.*

than a year later, they were released to the United States in exchange for 53 million dollars' worth of medicine and food. Fidel was considered an even greater hero than before. And the U.S. defeat at the Bay of Pigs led to the most dangerous confrontation of the Cold War.

BUILDUP TO CRISIS

At the end of 1961, Fidel announced to the world that Cuba was a Marxist-Leninist state, a Communist nation like the Soviet Union. Early the next year, President Kennedy expanded the trade embargo, banning all exports to Cuba except food and medicine. Imports from Cuba were also forbidden, including goods made in other countries from Cuban materials.

Fidel was convinced that the United States still posed a threat to Cuba's national security. He assumed that the Kennedy administration would organize another invasion like the Bay of Pigs, and he had to be ready. Khrushchev promised to protect Cuba and agreed to sell Fidel weapons. The Soviet premier arranged to supply Cuba with intermediate-range nuclear missiles, which would put the eastern United States within range of a nuclear attack.

The U.S. government learned in July 1962 that the Soviets had started shipping missiles to Cuba. In August, U.S. U-2 spy planes flying over the island spotted missile sites being constructed. The Kennedy administration warned the Soviet Union that bringing missiles into Cuba would provoke the United States. On

IRBM LAUNCH SITE NO 1
GUANAJAY, CUBA
23 OCTOBER 1962

BATCH PLANTS

PRE-FAB CONSTRUCTION MATERIALS

NUCLEAR STORAGE BUNKER

LAUNCH PAD

CONTROL BUILDING

PROTECTED VEHICLE POSITIONS

LAUNCH PAD

By building a missile base in Cuba, above, *the Soviet Union was ready to strike the United States quickly if the United States attacked the Soviet Union from U.S. nuclear bases in Turkey.*

October 14, a U.S. U-2 plane spotted Soviet missiles in western Cuba. Kennedy demanded that they be removed. Khrushchev refused.

THE MISSILE CRISIS

Kennedy considered whether to destroy the missiles by launching an air strike or by invading Cuba with ground forces. His advisers persuaded him to place a naval blockade on Cuba—surrounding the country with warships to prevent the delivery of more missiles.

TEETERING ON THE EDGE

any years after the Cuban missile crisis, documents revealed that the Soviets had several nuclear missiles in Cuba ready to strike if the United States invaded. Historians have also discovered that a horrifying incident almost occurred as U.S. warships trailed Soviet submarines off the Cuban coast.

On October 27, 1962, U.S. destroyers (small, fast warships) located a submerged Soviet submarine. They bombarded the sub with warning devices to force it to surface. An officer aboard the submarine said it was like "sitting in a metal barrel, which somebody is constantly blasting with a sledgehammer." After four hours, the commander decided that the war had started and ordered a nuclear-tipped torpedo to be fired. Luckily, another officer convinced him to reverse his order. The submarine rose to the surface instead. If the torpedo had been fired, the United States would have retaliated. A nuclear war would have started.

Kennedy warned Khrushchev that U.S. forces would seize any weapons the Soviets might try to deliver.

On October 22, the president announced on national television that the Soviet Union had positioned nuclear missiles in Cuba. Kennedy declared, "It shall be the policy of this nation to regard any nuclear missile launched from Cuba as an attack by the Soviet Union on the United States, requiring full retaliatory response on the Soviet Union." U.S. submarines went out to sea, bombers took to the sky, and ballistic missiles were prepared for firing. For several anxious days, the world teetered on the brink of nuclear war as the two superpowers faced off. People were terrified that World War III was about to start and they would die in a nuclear holocaust.

Tensions mounted as angry negotiations took place between the two world leaders. On October 27, a U.S. U-2 spy plane accidentally flew into Soviet airspace and another was shot down over Cuba. The next day, Khrushchev agreed to remove all missiles in return for a U.S. guarantee not to invade Cuba. Kennedy accepted. Kennedy also agreed in secret to remove U.S. missiles from a base in Turkey. (At the time, the Soviet Union shared a border with Turkey and felt threatened by the missiles there.) Though the missiles were never actually removed from Turkey, the crisis was over.

Fidel didn't know about Khrushchev's decision until he heard it on the radio, along with everyone else. Enraged, he refused to cooperate when the head of the United Nations met with him to verify that the missiles were being taken apart. But U.S. air inspections revealed that they were being removed, and the naval blockade of Cuba was lifted.

Castro toured the Soviet Union in 1963, receiving a warm welcome—and a warm hat.

Chapter **SEVEN**

COMMUNIST CUBA

AFTER THE MISSILE CRISIS WAS RESOLVED, Khrushchev invited Castro to visit the Soviet Union to cement the friendship between their countries. The Cuban leader began a triumphant forty-day tour in May 1963. He met with Khrushchev and other high-ranking officials and visited fourteen cities, including Moscow. Dressed in his trademark olive green fatigues, Fidel received a hero's welcome as he reviewed military parades and gave speeches at sports stadiums, factories, battlefields, and town squares.

Soon after Fidel returned to Cuba, his mother died, and he joined the rest of the family in Birán for her funeral. He also spent time with Fidelito, who was sixteen and preparing to attend the University of Havana.

In the fall of 1963, Hurricane Flora, one of the worst storms of the century, devastated Cuba. Fidel threw himself into the relief effort, showing little concern for his own safety. His leadership in times of national crisis reminded Cubans that they were being educated, fed, housed, and protected as never before.

COMMUNISM, CUBAN STYLE

During his first months in power, Fidel learned that he could control government policy by bringing his ideas directly to the people, a technique he called "democracy...of the marketplace." Most Cubans adored him, and huge crowds gathered at rallies to listen to his long, complicated speeches. Fidel asked the people what they thought of his plans, and they approved them by chanting responses to his questions. Many of their chants became popular slogans heard all over Cuba: "Cuba, Yes; Yankees, No!"; "Motherland or Death, We Shall Win!"; "You are doing all right, Fidel!"

In October 1963, Fidel proposed a new law that further restricted individual land ownership, putting 70 percent of all land in Cuba under government control. The government also took over retail businesses, even street vendors of sandwiches and ice cream. In a speech at a mass rally, Fidel justified the new policy: "Are we going to construct socialism, or are we going to construct vending stands? . . . We did not make a Revolution here to establish the right to trade!" The crowd laughed, applauded, and shouted its approval, although state control of business soon led to even greater hardships.

Che Guevara was Fidel's enthusiastic partner in Cuba's transformation to Marxism, but Che grew to distrust the Soviet Union as much as he did the United States. Che sharply criticized the Soviets for being timid in international affairs and for trying to dominate developing countries. As Fidel drew closer to the Soviets and became a classic Cuban dictator, Che was one of the few independent voices left in the government. But in April 1965, Che gave up his Cuban citizenship and left the country for good. He wanted to help lead revolutionary movements in other countries.

By the mid-1960s, Castro's Cuba was experiencing many hardships and the revolution showed signs of decay, as Time *magazine described it in October 1965.*

Castro speaks with members of the Young Pioneers. This youth program was designed to train Cuba's young people to support the revolution.

He was later captured and executed while trying to lead a rebellion against the Bolivian government.

After Che's death, Fidel praised him for his dedication to improving the lives of all Cubans. The official slogan of the Young Pioneers, Cuba's government-sponsored youth organization, became "We will be like Che."

In 1966 U.S. president Lyndon Johnson outlawed food shipments to any country that sold or shipped goods to Cuba, with a few exceptions. The expansion of the U.S. trade embargo and Fidel's mismanagement of the economy led Cuba to the brink of collapse. In 1968 the Soviet Union withheld oil shipments and delayed signing a new trade agreement. Fidel had annoyed Soviet leaders by jailing Cuban Communists who disagreed with him. The Soviets were also angry because Fidel was encouraging armed rebellion in several developing countries. Cuba was plunged into its worst crisis since the revolution. To obtain the aid he needed, Fidel was forced to cooperate with the Soviet leadership by suspending his calls for revolution around the world.

A NEW CONSTITUTION

Fidel's government approved a new constitution in 1976. It declared that Cuba was a socialist state and guaranteed all citizens jobs, medical care, education, food, clothing, and housing. It also praised Fidel as the one who would carry on the revolution, effectively naming him leader for life. Under the new constitution, Fidel had total power as president of Cuba, leader of the Cuban Communist Party, and commander in chief of the armed forces.

The "supreme organ of state power" was supposed to be the National Assembly of People's Power, which could pass, amend (change), and repeal (vote out) laws. Representatives were elected every five years. The National Assembly chose the members of the Council of State, which held the real power. Not surprisingly, Fidel was named president of the council while Raúl became first vice president.

ADVENTURES ABROAD

Fidel's ambitions extended beyond Cuba—he envisioned himself as a world leader. Beginning in 1962, he sent Cuban troops to fight alongside Marxist revolutionaries in various Latin American and African countries. He also encouraged thousands of Cuban civilians, including doctors, teachers, and construction workers to work in developing countries.

During the 1970s and 1980s, Cuban troops assisted Marxist guerrillas in Ethiopia, Nicaragua, Grenada, and Angola. More than 350,000 Cuban soldiers and 50,000 Cuban civilians served in Angola during its fifteen-year civil war. The revolutionary movement that overthrew the right-wing dictatorship in Nicaragua was founded in Cuba. Fidel became the new regime's main political and military backer. He also provided arms to guerrillas in El Salvador and Guatemala and helped establish a Marxist government on the Caribbean island of Grenada. As a result of his military and economic assistance to rebel forces in developing countries, Fidel became an important international leader.

RELATIONS WITH THE SUPERPOWERS

Between 1974 and 1980, U.S. presidents Richard Nixon, Gerald Ford, and Jimmy Carter all explored the possibility of improving relations with Cuba. But each time, Fidel angered the U.S. government by supporting Marxist revolutions in Latin America or Africa. The U.S.-Cuba trade embargo continued.

In January 1980, Celia Sánchez died of cancer. She had been Fidel's closest friend, adviser, and supporter since his days as a rebel leader in the Sierra Maestra.

With her, he could relax and be himself rather than the head of state and commander in chief. Fidel had lost his intellectual partner when Che Guevara was killed, but he lost his emotional partner when Celia died. She was the most important woman in his life and the most powerful woman in Cuba.

A few months later, President Carter announced that he planned to ease the trade embargo and end travel restrictions to Cuba. But when he casually mentioned that the United States would welcome Cuban political refugees with "open arms," Fidel flew into a rage. He allowed eleven thousand Cubans who had requested political asylum (protection from being arrested and the freedom to leave Cuba) to sail for the United States from the port of Mariel. Over the

"Marielitos" land in Florida in April 1980. President Carter had promised to welcome all Cuban refugees into the United States.

next five months, Fidel emptied the jails of criminals and other "antisocial elements," rounded up thousands of his critics, and forced them all to leave on boats from Mariel.

In the end, the Carter administration had to admit more than 120,000 of the so-called Marielitos, and Fidel got rid of his critics and criminals. The U.S. government retaliated by leaving the embargo and travel restrictions in place. Seven years later, Cuba took back about 2,500 Marielitos with histories of mental illness or criminal records and 4,000 others convicted of crimes in the United States.

President Ronald Reagan, who defeated Jimmy Carter in the 1980 election, was much more hostile toward Castro than Carter had been. Reagan disapproved of the Cuban leader's support for Communist governments in Central America and the Caribbean. Reagan sent troops to Grenada to fight the Marxist regime there, and he approved Radio Martí, a Miami-based radio station that broadcast anti-Castro propaganda to Cuba.

Cuba and the Soviet Union remained close allies until the mid-1980s. Soviet economic aid to Cuba reached five billion dollars a year, and nearly 80 percent of Cuba's trade was with the Soviet Union and its allies. But when Mikhail Gorbachev became head of the Soviet government in 1985, Cuban-Soviet relations began to cool. While Fidel remained a dedicated Marxist, Gorbachev began to experiment with a free-market economy and overhaul the Soviet political system. He was unwilling and unable to continue financing Cuba's state-controlled, inefficient economy. Gorbachev, who hoped to improve his country's relations with the United States, also criticized Cuba's interventions in other countries.

Fidel publicly condemned Gorbachev's reforms and his abandonment of revolutionary principles. The world was changing, and Cuba was being left behind.

Despite shifting political tides around the world in the early 1990s, Castro still clung to his belief in Communism.

Chapter **EIGHT**

A DECADE OF HARDSHIPS

BETWEEN **1989** AND **1991,** DRAMATIC POLITICAL changes rocked the Soviet Union and the Communist nations of eastern Europe. Soviet citizens voted in their first free election since 1918 and defeated the Communists. People in Russia and the other Soviet republics wanted the kinds of freedoms found in Western countries. As a result, the Soviet Union broke apart into separate nations. Communist governments also collapsed in other eastern European countries, including Hungary, Poland, and Czechoslovakia.

The breakup of the Soviet Union had a severe and immediate impact on Cuba. The country lost its most important trading partner and more than five billion dollars a year in assistance. As one historian noted,

Cuba was isolated, "a lone socialist island in a capitalist sea." Fidel faced a huge challenge. He had to find new sources of economic support in the capitalist world of Western nations, including his old enemy, the United States.

THE SPECIAL PERIOD

In 1990 Fidel declared a "Special Period in Peacetime," a sort of economic state of emergency that lasted ten years. Without the Soviets, Cuba had no place to sell its products and nowhere to get the raw materials it needed for industry. As a result, many factories shut down. Soviet-made products such as cars and televisions, as well as essential supplies of grain, food, and consumer goods were no longer available. Because of the drop in oil imports, there wasn't enough oil to make electricity. Blackouts occurred for up to sixteen hours a day.

Because of gas shortages, buses ran much less often and fuel for cars was scarce. Cubans had to depend on walking and biking for transportation. The government bought a million Chinese bicycles and distributed them throughout Cuba. "In nearly empty streets, the few cars and buses were surrounded by swarms of bicycles," wrote a reporter visiting Havana. In the countryside, farmers used plows pulled by oxen instead of tractors.

The worst hardship for the Cuban people was the extreme shortage of food and everyday necessities, espe-

Bicycles are one of the most common ways for Cubans to get from place to place.

cially during the first three years of the Special Period. Although Cuba had large areas of fertile land, it was too heavily planted with sugarcane. The people desperately needed fresh vegetables, fruits, and meat instead.

NEVER ENOUGH

Shortly after the 1959 revolution, Fidel had introduced a system of rationing (distribution of shares of food and other provisions) to guarantee that all Cubans would have basic necessities. Every household had a coupon book, and although people had to wait in lines every day to buy food and other products, everyone could get enough. And the prices were very low.

During the Special Period, however, the supply of goods dwindled. Fidel had to cut rations again and again. Cubans spent entire days waiting, but often they couldn't get what they needed. Meat, butter, soap,

and other staples became scarce and almost disappeared. Rations that were supposed to last a family
for a month ran out after only a week or two. People
were hungry and became malnourished.

The United States had imposed the first trade
restrictions on Cuba in 1960. The hope was that
Cubans would blame Castro's government for shortages of food and goods and turn against him. Thirty
years later, when the Soviet Union cut its support, the
U.S. government passed laws tightening the embargo.
As with the original embargo, the aim of the tighter
restrictions was to force Cuba's economy to collapse—
and Fidel's regime with it.

In 1992 President George H. W. Bush closed U.S.
airports and seaports to the planes and ships of countries that carried Cuban goods or passengers. Congress passed the Cuban Democracy Act, reducing U.S.
economic aid to countries that traded with Cuba.
Divisions of U.S. companies that operated in foreign
countries were also forbidden to trade with Cuba. The
act provoked international protest, and the United
Nations demanded an end to the embargo. Opponents
of the embargo argued that it only caused hardship
and suffering for the Cuban people while failing to
dislodge Castro from power.

BETTER TIMES FOR SOME

The desperate situation began to change in 1993,
when Fidel allowed Cubans to open some small

private businesses. Farmers were permitted to sell surplus food directly to consumers. Before 1993 people who earned extra money had to give most of it to the government. But under the new laws, Cubans could keep all their earnings. And businesses could accept U.S. dollars, which had a lot more buying power than Cuban pesos. Pesos were worth less than dollars because pesos couldn't be used to buy products from other countries, while dollars were accepted everywhere in the world. Even in Cuba, pesos bought very little.

The growing dollar economy had the effect of creating two classes of workers. Those who worked for the government—the majority—were paid in pesos and therefore were poorer and less privileged. Government employees, including teachers, doctors, lawyers, scientists, and police officers, earned only 350 to 500 pesos (seventeen to twenty-five dollars) a month.

Self-employed Cubans were paid in dollars and could afford to buy better food and goods. People who worked in the tourism industry, such as taxi drivers, waiters, and bartenders, earned a good living—sometimes more in a day than the monthly wage for state workers. For example, an artist could sell a painting to a tourist for twenty-five dollars and earn as much in a few hours as a doctor earned in a month. Many government employees quit their jobs and started private businesses. And many people who had full-time government jobs were self-employed on the side.

During the Special Period, most Cubans preferred to shop at the well-stocked and neatly organized dollar stores, above.

Cubans who were paid in pesos had to buy what they needed at peso stores, where the shelves were often nearly empty. Workers who earned dollars shopped at dollar stores, which accepted only dollars but were well stocked with food and products that had become scarce, such as soap, cosmetics, and deodorant. Many Cubans received dollars from family and friends who lived in the United States. Cuban Americans were allowed to visit their relatives in Cuba once a year. They brought packages of food and supplies and suitcases stuffed with cash.

TOURISM AND TRADE

Before the revolution, Cuba's biggest source of revenue besides sugar was tourism. After Fidel took over, he closed all the tourist hotels and casinos. When Soviet support vanished, however, Fidel realized that he would have to reopen Cuba to tourism.

By the end of the 1990s, tourists from Europe, Canada, and Mexico were spending almost two billion dollars a year in Cuba. Few of the tourists were American, since the trade embargo made it illegal for U.S. citizens to travel to Cuba. Some exceptions were allowed for educational, religious, and humanitarian groups. Tourism not only provided dollars to Cubans lucky enough to have jobs in the growing industry but also helped supply Fidel's government with much-needed dollars. Tourism quickly became Cuba's largest source of income.

Cubans were not allowed into tourist hotels and shops unless they worked there. Uniformed guards in hotel lobbies stopped any Cuban who tried to enter, even if accompanied by a tourist. Cubans could only peer into the tourist shops and see things they weren't allowed to buy, even if they had dollars.

Cuba's trade relations improved when Fidel invited foreign trade from other countries, such as Mexico and Canada, to replace the lost business with its former Communist partners. Cuba allowed billions in foreign investment and formed partnerships with international companies. For example, a Spanish company might build a luxury hotel, and the Cuban government would supply the workers. The Spanish firm paid the government in dollars for the workers' wages.

The government kept the dollars and paid the workers in pesos. In this way, dollars were pumped into the Cuban system.

LIFE REMAINS DIFFICULT

By the mid-1990s, the Cuban economy was slowly recovering, Cubans were becoming more optimistic, and Cuban American relations seemed to be improving. But in February 1996, the Cuban military shot down two U.S. civilian aircraft piloted by members of a Cuban American exile group. Cuba claimed that the planes were in Cuban airspace, but it was unclear which side was right. In retaliation, the U.S. Congress called for President Bill Clinton to sign the Helms-Burton Act into law. The law tightened the trade embargo even more.

The restrictions were so extreme that former president Jimmy Carter said, "I think of all the things that have ever been done in my country, this is the stupidest." Many U.S. allies became so angry that they sided with Cuba. The Helms-Burton Act actually helped Fidel, because Cubans rallied to support him.

Pope John Paul II, leader of the Roman Catholic faith, paid a special four-day visit to Cuba in January 1998. Cuba had been a Catholic country before the revolution. When Fidel first took power, he discouraged religious practices, but by the 1990s, he had become more tolerant. He invited the pope to visit and arranged for extensive media coverage. Fidel

Pope John Paul II traveled to Cuba in 1998. Both the pope and Castro viewed the visit as a political opportunity.

hoped that John Paul's presence would help keep Cubans united behind the government.

Unfortunately, the pope's visit couldn't help solve the problems caused by years of dissatisfaction and hardship. Serious crimes such as robbery, which had almost disappeared after the revolution, became more common. Drugs were sold openly on the streets, and some women turned to prostitution. Fidel still ruled, but Cuba was not the utopia he'd imagined.

After more than four decades as ruler of Cuba, Castro shows no sign of stepping down or veering from his original vision of a socialist nation.

Chapter **NINE**

FIDEL FOREVER?

THE NEW CENTURY OPENED WITH A DRAMATIC EVENT that reflected U.S.-Cuba relations and was a reminder of Fidel's past. In November 1999, the U.S. Coast Guard rescued Elián González, a five-year-old Cuban boy, from drowning in the Atlantic Ocean off the coast of Florida. His mother had taken him aboard a boat of refugees headed for the United States and, they hoped, a better life. But the boat sank, and Elián's mother drowned. Elián clung to a tire for two days before he was rescued and taken to Miami. Family members there were determined to keep the boy, but his father, who lived in Cuba, wanted him back. Elián became a symbol of U.S. opposition to Castro's Cuba.

Lincoln Diaz-Balart, a congressman from Florida, led the crusade to keep Elián in the United States. Diaz-Balart took a special interest in the case, because his aunt is Fidel's ex-wife Mirta. Diaz-Balart knew about her losing battle for custody of her son Fidelito, his first cousin. After six months of legal challenges and daily media coverage, President Clinton sent federal officers to remove Elián from his relatives' home by force. The boy was reunited with his father, and they returned to Cuba. Once again, Fidel won international sympathy for Cuba at the expense of the United States.

CONTEMPORARY CUBA

Despite the tough times Cubans have endured, their vibrant culture rémains a source of pride and enjoyment. Cubans are friendly and generous, charming and tolerant. Foreign visitors, including Americans, are welcomed. In Cuba the air hums with music and the streets are alive with brightly colored art. Dancing is a national pastime, and any occasion can turn into a party.

Education, including college, is free in Cuba, and the literacy rate is among the highest in the world. Cubans also receive free health care. The average life span is long, and the number of infant deaths is very low. Cuba has more doctors per person than the United States, although the Special Period caused a serious shortage of medicines.

More than 60 percent of Cuba's 11 million people were born after the revolution, so Fidel is the only leader they have ever known. Unlike their parents, this generation didn't live under Batista's corrupt rule. They haven't faced the threat of a U.S. invasion or known the excitement of working together to bring about social change. Like young people everywhere, they want to find good jobs and enjoy life. They care more about their own futures than that of the Communist Party. Young adults in Cuba are more likely to go into business for themselves than work for the government, and they enthusiastically spend money, especially on U.S. products.

Conditions in Cuba have progressed since the Special Period. Foreign investment has slowly improved the economy and raised the standard of living, though shortages still occur. Despite a better standard of living, thousands of people still try to leave Cuba for the United States. They set out in all kinds of homemade contraptions, from makeshift rafts to "pontoon boats"— 1950s cars and trucks with floats attached.

The U.S. government has changed its immigration policy since the early days of Fidel's regime. These days, Cubans who are picked up at sea are sent back to Cuba. Although the United States grants more than twenty thousand visas a year to Cubans who apply to emigrate from Cuba, the demand is far greater than the allotted quota. For example, recently more than 500,000 Cubans applied for visas in a single year.

No Dissent Allowed

In Castro's Cuba, the Communist Party is the only political party allowed. Citizens don't have many of the rights Americans take for granted: they can't protest government actions, travel freely, meet with anyone they want, or write or speak whatever they choose. It's a crime to spread "unauthorized news"—anything the government hasn't approved—or insult patriotic symbols.

The Varela Project, a reform effort led by Oswaldo Payá, challenged the government's restriction of civil and political rights. In May 2001, Payá delivered a petition signed by more than eleven thousand citizens to the National Assembly (Cuba's legislature). The petition called for free and fair elections, freedom of the press, and pardons for political prisoners. Fidel's government responded by circulating its own petition in support of the existing system, and Fidel claimed to have gathered over eight million signatures in two days. Then the National Assembly approved a change to the constitution that made socialism "irrevocable" (unchangeable). Many political dissidents (those who disagree with the government) were arrested during the next few months.

The United Nations has passed many resolutions criticizing Cuba's human rights violations. Cubans who have done nothing illegal can be arrested for being "dangerous." It's difficult for someone who is accused of a crime against the government to get a fair trial, because the laws favor the government.

In March 2003, the Cuban government arrested nearly eighty people, including political dissidents, human rights activists, and independent journalists. They received harsh sentences ranging from twelve to twenty-five years in prison. The prisoners live in over-crowded cells, don't get enough to eat, and receive poor medical care. If they try to publicize their mistreatment, they are physically abused and put in solitary confinement. The government has not allowed international human rights groups to investigate the situation.

AN UNCERTAIN FUTURE

Ten U.S. presidents, from Dwight Eisenhower to George W. Bush, and forty years of embargoes have failed to remove Fidel from power. Although the U.S. government has made peace with other former enemies, its relations with Cuba remain hostile.

Cuban Americans have worked successfully to keep pressure on Fidel. Their votes for anti-Castro candidates in the United States have played an important role in presidential and congressional elections. In June 2004, President Bush expanded the trade and travel bans, hoping to force Cuba to allow free elections, reform its Communist economic system, and get rid of Fidel. Under the new law, Cuban exiles are allowed to visit family members in Cuba only once every three years rather than once a year. They can spend only fifty dollars each day they're there. The law also makes it much more difficult for U.S. tourists to visit Cuba.

Meanwhile, Fidel is almost eighty years old but shows no sign of loosening his grip on power. Although his hair and beard are mostly gray, he's still physically and mentally fit. He rides an exercise bike every day and keeps his mind active by reading widely.

Fidel never remarried and has no contact with Mirta, who lives in Spain with her second husband. No one has replaced Celia Sánchez as his close friend and confidant. Fidel loves his son and sees him whenever possible, but both men lead busy lives. Fidelito is married, with two children, and is a respected physicist and head of the Cuban Nuclear Commission.

Fidel enjoys long discussions with visitors from around the world. The American playwright Arthur Miller visited Cuba in early 2000 with a small group of writers. Much to Miller's surprise, the Cuban leader invited the group to dinner. He kept everyone at the table until two in the morning while he showed off his knowledge of a variety of topics. Miller finally got permission to leave by explaining that he was old and tired and needed to go to bed. As a parting gift, Fidel gave each guest a bag of his special vitamins.

The future of Cuba's government after Fidel is uncertain. His brother Raúl is his official successor, but Raúl is seventy-three and has none of his older brother's charisma or leadership skills. A few younger politicians, including Ricardo Alarcón, president of the National Assembly, are sometimes mentioned as possible successors. Whoever succeeds Fidel will need the support of the army, because it is the strongest, most organized force in Cuba.

An opposition movement exists in Cuba, but the government has jailed its most outspoken members. And most Cubans, even Castro's opponents, would be against a takeover by Cuban Americans who hate Fidel. Any attempt to overthrow him might cause a civil war.

Some political analysts believe that if the U.S. trade embargo were lifted, the standard of living in Cuba would improve and Cubans would be less willing to tolerate Fidel's political and economic restrictions. Other analysts still believe that enacting even stricter U.S. measures against Cuba is the only way to spur Cubans to rise up against Fidel.

Fidel is proud, stubborn, and certain that only he knows what's best for Cuba. Although most world leaders have given up on Marxism, he clings to the policies that have caused so much economic hardship and loss of personal freedom for his people. He has said, "I have no choice but to continue being a Communist. . . . If I'm told 98 percent of the people no longer believe in the Revolution, I'll continue to fight. If I'm told I'm the only one who believes in it, I'll continue."

SOURCES

7–8   Fidel Castro, "Letter from Fidel Castro, Age 12, to
President Franklin D. Roosevelt, 11/06/1940," *National
Archives and Records Administration*, n.d. http://arcweb
.archives.gov/arc/arch_results_detail.jsp?&pg=3&si=0&nh
=100&st=b (September 14, 2004).

14   Fidel Castro, *My Early Years* (New York: Ocean Press,
1998), 68–69.

15   Tad Szulc, *Fidel: A Critical Portrait* (New York:
HarperCollins, 1987), 109.

17   Ibid., 113.

17   Ibid., 114.

18–19   Castro, *My Early Years*, 70.

19   Ibid., 75.

21   Ibid., 3.

25   Ibid., 84.

25   Szulc, *Fidel: A Critical Portrait*, 145.

27   Ibid., 153.

30   Robert E. Quirk, *Fidel Castro* (New York: W. W. Norton &
Co., 1993), 24.

32   Szulc, *Fidel: A Critical Portrait*, 177.

32   Ibid., 179.

35   Ibid., 193.

35   Ibid., 197.

44–45   Fidel Castro, "History Will Absolve Me," *Fidel Castro
History Archive*, n.d., http://www.marxists.org/history
/cuba/archive/castro/1953/10/16.htm (July 29, 2004).

45   Szulc, *Fidel: A Critical Portrait*, 306.

51   Ibid., 336.

53   Ibid., 340.

56   Christopher P. Baker, *Moon Handbooks: Cuba,* 2nd ed.
(Emeryville, CA: Avalon Travel Publishing, 1999), 40.

59   Fidel Castro, "Against Complacency," COBC, January 9,
1959.

64   Szulc, *Fidel: A Critical Portrait*, 489.

67   Baker, *Moon Handbooks: Cuba*, 115.

76 Knight Ridder/Tribune News Service, Matthew Hay
    Brown, "Former U.S., Soviet, Cuban Officials Offer
    Glimpse into Cuban Missile Crisis." *Orlando Sentinel*,
    October 11, 2002.
76 Baker, *Moon Handbooks: Cuba*, 46.
80 Szulc, *Fidel: A Critical Portrait*, 469.
80 Ibid., 609.
85 Ibid., 645.
90 Baker, *Moon Handbooks: Cuba*, 54.
90 James Wiley, "Havana by Bicycle during Cuba's Special
    Period," *Focus*, Winter 1993, 1.
96 Baker, *Moon Handbooks: Cuba*, 57.
105 Ibid., 68.

SELECTED BIBLIOGRAPHY

Baker, Christopher P. *Moon Handbooks: Cuba*. 2nd ed.
    Emeryville, CA: Avalon Travel Publishing, 1999.
Castro, Fidel. "History Will Absolve Me." *Fidel Castro History
    Archive*. n.d. http://www.marxists.org/history/cuba
    /archive/castro/1953/10/16.htm (July 1, 2004).
———. *My Early Years*. New York: Ocean Press, 1998.
"The Cuban Missile Crisis, October 18–29, 1962." *History Out Loud*.
    October 8, 1997. http:/www.hpol.org/jfk/cuban (July 1, 2004).
Knight Ridder/Tribune News Service. Matthew Hay Brown.
    "Former U.S., Soviet, Cuban Officials Offer Glimpse into
    Cuban Missile Crisis." *Orlando Sentinel*. October 11, 2002.
Miller, Arthur. "A Visit with Fidel." *Nation*, January 12–19, 2004.
Quirk, Robert E. *Fidel Castro*. New York: W. W. Norton & Co.,
    1993.
Ripley, C. Peter. *Conversations with Cuba*. Athens: University of
    Georgia Press, 2001.
Szulc, Tad. *Fidel: A Critical Portrait*. New York: HarperCollins, 1987.

FURTHER READING
AND WEBSITES

Behnke, Alison, and Victor Manuel Valens. *Cooking the Cuban Way*. Minneapolis: Lerner Publications Company, 2004.

Bentley, Judith. *Fidel Castro of Cuba*. Englewood Cliffs, NJ: Julian Messner, 1991.

Beyer, Don E. *Castro!* New York: Franklin Watts, 1993.

Campbell, Kumari. *Cuba in Pictures*. Minneapolis: Lerner Publications Company, 2005.

Morrison, Marion. *Cuba*. New York: Children's Press, 1999.

Salas, Osvaldo. *Fidel's Cuba: A Revolution in Pictures*. New York: Thunder's Mouth Press, 1998.

Che Guevara Internet Archive
http://www.marxists.org/archive/guevara/
Read Guevara's biography, view images, and listen to speeches at this website.

CubaNet
http://www/cubanet.org/cubanews.html.
This website collects articles from many different sources to provide current information and news about Cuba.

Fidel Castro History Archive
http://www.marxists.org/history/cuba/archive/castro/
This website contains a collection of transcripts from some of Castro's speeches as well as some of his writings.

INDEX

OTHER TITLES FROM LERNER AND A&E®:

Arnold Schwarzenegger
Ariel Sharon
Arthur Ashe
The Beatles
Benjamin Franklin
Bill Gates
Bruce Lee
Carl Sagan
Chief Crazy Horse
Christopher Reeve
Colin Powell
Daring Pirate Women
Edgar Allan Poe
Eleanor Roosevelt
George Lucas
George W. Bush
Gloria Estefan
Jack London
Jacques Cousteau
Jane Austen
Jesse Owens
Jesse Ventura
Jimi Hendrix
John Glenn
Hillary Rodham Clinton
Latin Sensations
Legends of Dracula

Legends of Santa Claus
Louisa May Alcott
Madeleine Albright
Malcolm X
Mark Twain
Maya Angelou
Mohandas Gandhi
Mother Teresa
Nelson Mandela
Oprah Winfrey
Osama bin Laden
Princess Diana
Queen Cleopatra
Queen Elizabeth I
Queen Latifah
Rosie O'Donnell
Saddam Hussein
Saint Joan of Arc
Thurgood Marshall
Tiger Woods
Tony Blair
Vladimir Putin
William Shakespeare
Wilma Rudolph
Women in Space
Women of the Wild West
Yasser Arafat

ABOUT THE AUTHORS

Ellen R. Butts is a co-author of several biographies and magazine articles. She has worked as an editor for many years, as well as a research and reference librarian. She also volunteers as an ESL teacher.

Joyce R. Schwartz has taught both elementary and middle school science. She has coauthored several biographies for children and is currently a tour guide at the National Gallery of Art.

PHOTO ACKNOWLEDGMENTS

Photographs used with the permission of: © Claudia Daut/Reuters/CORBIS, p. 2; © AP\Wide World Photos, pp. 6, 10, 17, 22, 25, 70, 85; National Archives, p. 8 [NWDNS-306-NT-165-319C]; © Time Life Pictures/Getty Images, pp. 32, 62, 81, 88; © AFP/Getty Images, pp. 36, 41, 98; © Getty Images, p. 59; © Barbara Gordon, p. 34; © Robert van der Hilst/CORBIS, p. 46; © Bettmann/CORBIS, pp. 48, 63, 73, 82; Archives and Special Collections Department, Otto G. Richter Library, University of Miami, p. 51; Library of Congress, pp. 56, 60 [LC-USZ62-95451], 69 [LC-USZ62-127229], 78 [LC-USZ62-128592]; The John F. Kennedy Library, p. 75 [PX66-20:19]; © John Kreul/Independent Picture Service, pp. 91, 94; © Reuters/CORBIS, p. 97.

Cover photos (hard cover and soft cover): front, © Francoise de Mulder/CORBIS; back, © AP\Wide World Photos.